MINECRAFT

ENGLISH
OFFICIAL WORKBOOK
AGES 5-6

**JON GOULDING
AND DAN WHITEHEAD**

INTRODUCTION

HOW TO USE THIS BOOK

Welcome to an exciting educational experience! Your child will go on a series of adventures through the amazing world of Minecraft, improving their written English skills along the way. Matched to the National Curriculum for writing for ages 5–6 (Year 1), this workbook takes your child into fascinating landscapes where our heroes Eva and Tom embark on building projects and daring treasure hunts…all while keeping those pesky mobs at bay!

As each adventure unfolds, your child will complete topic-based questions worth a certain number of emeralds . These can then be 'traded in' on the final page. The more challenging questions are marked with this icon to stretch your child's learning. Answers are included at the back of the book.

Note: While using this book, your child is likely to need some adult support, such as in reading explanations to them and giving any further help as necessary.

MEET OUR HEROES

Eva is an eager adventurer who just wants to get out and explore the world. Finding cool new places and unearthing rare loot are what she loves best. She is a naturally gifted fighter because her adventures take her into some dangerous spots, but she still likes to come back and chill out with her best friend, Tom.

Tom has seen lots of biomes during his adventures but he doesn't go searching for glory and treasure. His main interest is designing and building, so he is always looking out for cool new blocks to use in his creations. If he has to battle zombies and skeletons to get them, he is ready!

First published in 2021 by Collins
An imprint of HarperCollins*Publishers*
1 London Bridge Street, London, SE1 9GF

HarperCollins*Publishers*
1st Floor, Watermarque Building, Ringsend Road, Dublin 4, Ireland

Publisher: Fiona McGlade
Authors: Jon Goulding and Dan Whitehead
Project management: Richard Toms
Design: Ian Wrigley and Sarah Duxbury
Typesetting: Nicola Lancashire at Rose and Thorn Creative Services

Special thanks to Alex Wiltshire, Sherin Kwan and Marie-Louise Bengtsson at Mojang and the team at Farshore

Production: Karen Nulty

ISBN 978-0-00-846280-2
British Library Cataloguing in Publication Data.
A CIP record of this book is available from the British Library.
1 2 3 4 5 6 7 8 9 10
Printed in the United Kingdom

MOJANG STUDIOS

MIX
Paper from responsible source
FSC
www.fsc.org
FSC™ C007454

This book is produced from independently certified FSC™ paper to ensure responsible forest management.

For more information visit: www.harpercollins.co.uk/green

CONTENTS

TRANSCRIPTION AND SPELLING

STARTING POINT

Welcome to the plains! Lots of Minecraft adventures start here but that does not mean it is somewhere to relax. You might find a friendly village among the grass, flowers and oak trees but at night the creepers, skeletons and zombies appear and you should definitely have a safe shelter ready when that happens.

LET THE ADVENTURE BEGIN!

Eva stretches and wonders what the day will bring. It is time to set off on her adventure. Eva has until dark to find enough wood and stone to build a house and some weapons to defend herself. While she goes, Tom stays behind to work on his house. Ready? Here we go!

DIFFERENT SPELLINGS FOR SOUNDS: VOWEL SOUNDS

The vowels – a, e, i, o and u – can make short sounds as in c_a_t, p_e_n, t_i_n, c_o_t and c_u_p. They can also make long sounds, usually when combined with other letters.

Eva begins her mission but she must hurry before the sun sets.

1

Complete these sentences with a word from the box. The words contain different long *a* sounds.

day	safe	plains	make

a) Eva needs wood to **m** a **k** **e** a shelter.

b) There is lots of grass on the **p** l **ai** n **s**.

c) It is best to collect wood during the **d** **ay**.

d) A house will keep Eva **s** a **f** **e** from dangerous mobs at night.

2

Use the correct long e sound from the box to complete the word in each sentence.

ea	e – e	ee	ie

a) Eva can **s** e e a village in the distance.

b) She is hungry but will not e a **t** grass.

c) There are not many things growing on **th** e **s** e **plains**.

d) It would be wrong to be a **th** i e **f** and steal wood from the village.

Eva reaches the village but will the villagers help her?

3

Draw lines to match each word with a long *i* sound to the correct sentence.

It will go dark at *night*	lives
Eva will need somewhere to *lie* down.	night
She has *tried* to craft a bed.	lie
The villagers are busy with their own *lives*.	tried

4

Complete these sentences with a word from the box. The words contain different long *o* sounds.

goal	borrow	biome	foe

a) The plains *b i* o *m* e is dangerous at night.

b) Eva makes it her *g* oa *l* to build a house soon.

c) She does not want to meet a *f* oe.

d) The villagers let her *borr* ow some wood.

Eva has some wood and can begin crafting. She picks a great spot for her first shelter.

5

Complete the words with the correct long *u* sound from the box.

ue	ew	u – e	oo

a) The blocks of wood are a **c** u **b** e shape.

b) There are a **f** e w horses nearby.

c) Eva can see some **bl** u e water.

d) Eva needs to find **f** oo **d**.

6

 Write the noun (the naming word) from each sentence. Underline the long vowel sound in the word you write.

a) There could be rain soon.　　　Soon

b) A sturdy home helps to protect you.　　helps

c) The sea is close by.　　close

d) It is a lovely sight.　　sight

WORDS WITH THE LONG *ER, IR* AND *UR* SOUND, AND THE LAZY *ER*

The spelling patterns *er*, *ir* and *ur* often make a long sound as in the words h<u>er</u>, g<u>ir</u>l, and b<u>ur</u>st. The spelling *er* can also make a different sound known as a 'schwa' (or sometimes called a 'lazy' sound) when the *er* is said fully (for example, in summ<u>er</u> the *er* makes an *uh* sound). When practising spelling these words, it helps to say the word slowly and over-pronounce the ending by saying the long *er* sound.

It will soon be time to build a shelter but Eva is starving. Time for dinner! While she finds food, answer these questions.

Draw lines to join each word to the correct spelling of the long sound it contains.

shirt	verb	turn	her

| | er | | ur | | ir | |

Choose the correct word from the box to complete each sentence.

bird	first	stronger	survive

a) It is the ....*first*........ day of Eva's adventure in the plains biome.

b) She needs food to ....*Survive*........ .

c) She catches a chicken, which is a type of ....*Bird*........ .

d) The cooked meat will make her ....*Stronger*........ .

Eva starts building her house but keeps her eyes open for danger.

3

Add the correct sound to each word below. Use a long *er, ir* or *ur* sound.

a) If a zombie attacks then Eva could get **h u n t.**

b) She must stay **al e r t** at all times.

c) If she gets lost, she will be going round in **c i r cles**.

d) It is a good job she is an **exp e r t!**

4

Sort the words with the long *er* sound from those with the lazy ('schwa') *er* sound. Write them in the correct part of the table.

| under | shirt | spider | creeper | survival |
| occur | person | shelter | stronger | disturb |

Long *er* sound	Lazy *er* sound
	under shirt

5

Explain what you notice about the lazy *er* sound in the words in question 4.

DAYS OF THE WEEK

Each day of the week has a different spelling. Some are easier to spell than others but you must learn them all.

Safe in her new house, Eva starts to plan for the days ahead.

1

Unscramble all the letters for each day of the week. Write the correct spelling for each day.

ndaoMy **hurTsyad** **dendsWaye**

yadnuS **uTdesya** **iyadrF** **urStdaya**

2

Fill in the spaces to write the days of the week in the correct order.

Monday

Thursday

Saturday

There's always something to do. Eva is going to have a busy week. What is she going to do on each day?

3

Add the correct letters to complete each word.

a) Build a house on **M** .... **d** ....

b) Do some farming on **F** .... **ay**

c) Chill out on .... **un** .... **ay**

d) Go mining for ore on **T** .... **e** ....

e) Explore the mountains on **T** .... **r** ....

f) Hunt for diamonds on **Sa** .... **ay**

g) Meet Tom on **Wed** .... **day**

4

Complete the name of these days of the week.

a) .... **ue** ....   b) .... **rs** ....

c) .... **es** ....   d) .... **on** ....

5

What type of letter does the name of every day of the week begin with?

....

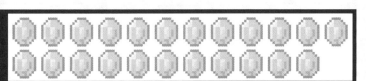

OR, ORE, AW AND AU SPELLINGS

The *or* sound in words can be spelled *or*, *ore*, *aw* and *au*.
It is important to learn the spelling of the different *or* sounds.

The next day, Eva sets out to look for some iron ore to craft weapons and armour. Answer these questions while she searches.

1

Find and copy all words containing the *or* sound from the two sentences below.

> *Eva spent all morning searching for ore.*
> *She had some before but wants more.*

....

....

2

Sort the words with the different *or* sounds into the correct parts of the table.

draw   pause   score   shore   dawn   haunt

ore words	*aw* words	*au* words

Eva finds enough iron ore to make a sword. Now she's looking for coal to make torches, but she's not alone. Watch out for that zombie!

3

Complete the gaps in the missing words.

a) Eva found some coal .... **r** ....

b) She used it to make a **t** .... **ch**.

c) Eva could see **h** .... **ses** on the plains.

d) Eva made an iron **sw** .... **d**.

4

Write the correct word containing an *or* sound in each space. Choose from the words in the box below.

torn	short	saw	wore	sword	more	spawn

Eva .... a zombie. It ....

.... clothes. Although she was .... of

strength, she took her .... and defeated the zombie. She hoped

.... would not .... nearby.

 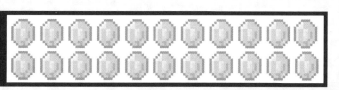

AR, ARE, AIR AND EAR SPELLINGS

The spellings *ar*, *are*, *air* and *ear* look similar but are often used for different sounds. The spellings *ar* and *are* make a long *r* sound as in c<u>ar</u> or the word <u>are</u>. The spelling *are* can also make the same sound as *air* and *ear* in words such as <u>air</u>, b<u>ear</u> and r<u>are</u>.

Eva defeats the zombie but it is a tough fight. She needs to rest and heal.

I

Copy the word from each sentence that contains the *ar* sound that is heard in the word *car*.

a) The zombie had started the fight. ....

b) The zombie hurt Eva's arm. ....

c) The wound could leave a scar. ....

d) It can be hard to survive at night. ....

2

Copy the word from each sentence that contains the *air* sound.

a) Eva escaped the zombie's lair. ....

b) Eva got quite a scare. ....

c) If only she had some armour to wear. ....

d) Eva was aware of the great danger. ....

Hungry, injured and far from home as night falls, Eva is in real trouble now. Be careful, Eva!

3

Complete each word with the correct *air* sound. Then put the words in the correct parts of the table.

shar____ f____ ir t____ ar sc____ re be____ r pa____ r

air words	*are* words	*ear* words

4

Write the correct word containing an *ar* or an *air* sound in each space of the passage below. Choose from the words in the box.

fair	hard	scared	apart	stared	large	dared

Sometimes it can be _____ to find food. Eva _____

at the land ahead of her. _____ from a few horses, she could see

nothing else. She was so low on health that she _____ not fight a

zombie or a creeper. She then saw a _____ spider. She didn't think

this was very _____ and she realised she was _____ .

COLOUR IN HOW MANY EMERALDS YOU EARNED

OW AND OU SPELLINGS

The spellings *ow* and *ou* can make different sounds but are also often used for the sound that is heard in the words *how* and *out*.

The mobs are everywhere now! Eva needs to escape. Maybe those buildings in the distance will help?

1

Draw lines to join each word with an *ow* or *ou* sound to the sentence it completes.

Eva could hear the _____ of a skeleton.	about
She needed to find shelter _____ .	now
It was _____ time she got to safety.	around
She looked _____ for somewhere.	sound

2

Complete each sentence with the correct word from the box that contains an *ow* or an *ou* sound.

cow	down	brown	outpost

a) Eva took out her saddle and rode away on a........................... horse.

b) Oh no! She spotted a pillager ....

c) Why couldn't it be a nice, friendly .... ?

d) She raced .... the hill away from the danger.

Eva gets away from the pillagers. Then she finds an interesting cave.

3

Look at each sentence and find the word with the *ow* or the *ou* sound.
Write the word and underline the *ow* or the *ou* sound as you write it.

a) Eva should have found more food. ....

b) She could ride around the cave. ....

c) Eva wanted to check it out. ....

d) Will she be wowed by the treasure inside? ....

4

♥ Read each word below. Say and write a sentence containing that word.

a) mouth

....

b) town

....

c) growl

....

d) count

....

COLOUR IN HOW MANY EMERALDS YOU EARNED

17

EAR AND ERE SPELLINGS

The spelling *ear* can make the *air* sound in words such as *ch<u>air</u>* (see page 14) but it can also be used to spell the sound that is heard in the word *dear* (and in the word *ear* itself). The spelling *ere* can make the same sound but can also make an *air* sound or even an *er* sound.

Before Eva can investigate the cave, she hears a familiar hissing sound close by. Oh no!

 1 ————————————————————————

Find and write the two words containing the sound heard in the word *ear* from the sentences below.

> *Eva knew there was a creeper nearby.*
> *She could hear it but for now she was safe.*

....

2 ————————————————————————

Sort these words into the two different sounds they contain.

| where | beard | here | hear | sphere | there |

air sound words	*ear* sound as in *dear*

Alone in the dark, with creepers closing in. What is Eva going to do?

3 ⬡⬡⬡⬡

Complete the gaps in the missing words.

a)   Eva could not see **wh** .... **r** .... the creeper was.

b)   She was sure it was **h** .... **r** .... before.

c)   She knew it must be **n** .... **r**.

d)   How many other creepers could **th** .... **r** .... be?

4 ⬡⬡⬡⬡

Choose the best word from the box to fill each space in these sentences.

nowhere   hear   nearby   were

Eva could .... *more creepers* ....

She looked but they .... *to be seen.*

 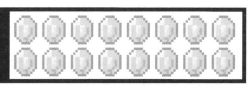

WORD ENDINGS

Some short words with a single vowel letter, such as *buzz*, have a double consonant at the end. The double letter is usually *ll*, *ff*, *ss*, *zz* or *ck* (representing the double *k* sound). Words such as *bank* have a single vowel followed by *nk* to give a distinct sound, while words such as *hutch* use *tch*. An *ee* sound at the end of words is usually spelled *y*, as in the word *happy*. A *v* sound at the end of words is often spelled *ve*, as in the word *live*.

The creepers are closing in. Will Eva fight or flee? Help her out by answering these questions.

1

Draw lines to match each word to its final sound.

| live | pull | snatch | honk | fizz | crack | welly |

| l | nk | z | ee | k | v | tch |

2

Add the correct sound to each word in the sentences below.

Choose from *ff*, *nk*, *tch* and *ve*.

a) Eva had to **thi** .... carefully to avoid the creepers.

b) She didn't want to **ha** .... another battle.

c) Eva ran **o** .... to avoid fighting the creepers.

d) She had to **ca** .... another horse.

The creepers are chasing Eva.

3

Complete each word with the correct two-letter ending. Then write each word in the correct part of the table.

Eva ran up a **hi**............. She tried to **tri**............. the creepers.

She heard a **hi**............. The creepers were far **o**............. now.

-ss ending	*-ll* ending	*-ff* ending	*-ck* ending

4

Create a sentence using each given word. Say the sentence out loud and then try to write it.

a) miss

....

b) smelly

....

c) move

....

d) fetch

....

COLOUR IN HOW MANY EMERALDS YOU EARNED

WH, PH AND K SPELLINGS

The spelling *wh* is sometimes used to make the *w* sound as heard in the word <u>w</u>in. The spelling *ph* is sometimes used to make an *f* sound as heard in the word *fit*. A *k* can be used for the *k* sound heard in the word <u>c</u>at, if it comes before *e*, *i* or *y*.

As the sun begins to rise, Eva leaves the creepers far behind and heads back home to meet Tom.

1

Draw lines to join each word to the sound it contains.

| whiff | phonics | king | dolphin | wheel | sketch |

| ph | k | wh |

2

Choose the best word from the box to complete each sentence. Use a capital letter on your chosen word if needed.

| which   phew   what   skin |

a) .... an adventure she had in the plains!

b) The creepers made Eva almost jump out of her ....

c) She wondered .... place they would visit next.

d) "............................., I survived!" said Eva.

COLOUR IN HOW MANY EMERALDS YOU EARNED

ADVENTURE ROUND-UP

AN ORE-SOME NIGHT!

What a wild night Eva had! Back in the house, she unloads all the ore she found on her adventure. Tom calls round and she tells him the whole story, including how she got some wood from the villagers and tamed horses. She tells him how she fought a zombie, sneaked past a pillager outpost and escaped from creepers.

CAVE CHALLENGE

"That sounds like quite an adventure!" says Tom.

"I just wish I'd had a chance to explore the cave I found," replies Eva.

"A cave?" asks Tom. "That sounds like just the sort of challenge I'm looking for! Mark it on the map for me and I'll check it out tomorrow."

And with that, Eva tucks into her well-earned dinner. Baked potato and mushroom stew. Yum!

VOCABULARY, GRAMMAR AND PUNCTUATION

TAKE CARE IN THE CAVES

Caves are great! You can't have a Minecraft adventure without venturing into these mysterious caverns, but every time you explore you are taking a big risk.

GOING DOWN

Caves might be full of precious and useful ore but they are also where you'll find all kinds of monstrous mobs lurking in the darkness, waiting to pounce. Craft your best gear, load up with torches and plunge into the depths!

MYSTERY OF THE DEEP

Eva's tale of the mysterious cave has filled Tom with excitement. What will he find deep inside? He sets off to discover the answer for himself...

SINGULAR AND PLURAL

Singular means one of something (for example: *a villager*). Plural means more than one (for example: *some villagers*). To make most words plural, you just need to add an *s* to the word. But watch out... you need to add *es* to make the plural of words that end in *x, ch, sh, s* and *z* (for example: *fox – foxes*; *church – churches*).

Tom waves goodbye to Eva and sets off to find the cave. On the way, he thinks about what might be waiting for him.

1

Write the plural of each highlighted word below.

a)   One **creeper**   →   Four ....

b)   One **witch**   →   Two ....

c)   One **bat**   →   Six ....

d)   One **block**   →   Many ....

2

Tick (✓) the correct word to complete each sentence.

a)   Tom wished he had a   **llama** ☐ **llamas** ☐   to carry any ore he might find.

b)   Eva had said the cave was near lots of spruce   **tree.** ☐ **trees.** ☐

c)   Tom hopes there will not be any   **zombies** ☐ **zombie** ☐   in the cave.

THE PREFIX *UN-*

Prefixes are added to the beginning of a word to change its meaning. Adding the prefix *un-* gives a word the opposite meaning. Be careful...the prefix *un-* cannot be added to every word.

Oops! Tom tries to remember Eva's directions to the cave but gets lost on the way. Help him out by answering the following questions.

1

Complete these prefix additions.

a) un- + happy = ...

b) un- + tidy   = ...

c) un- + do   = ...

d) un- + tie   = ...

2

Choose the best word from the box to complete each sentence.

unlucky   unsure   unwell   unable

a) Tom feels .... because he needs food and rest.

b) He is .... about where he is.

c) Tom worries that he will be .... to find the caves.

d) It would be .... if any zombies came along now.

Tom still cannot find the cave and the sun is setting. He quickly builds a shelter to hide from creepers.

3

Add the prefix *un-* to a word in each sentence to change the meaning.

a)   In his shelter, Tom is seen by any creepers.   ....

b)   It is very like Tom to be scared.   ....

c)   The way to the caves is known.   ....

d)   It seems so fair that he cannot find the cave.   ....

4

Look at these words. Which are correctly written with the *un-* prefix? Which are incorrectly written with the *un-* prefix? Write the words in the correct part of the table.

unlock   **unagree**   **untie**   **unappear**   **unfold**

unusual   **uncorrect**

Correct *un-* words	Incorrect *un-* words

ADDING ER, ED, EST AND ING TO WORDS

The ending *er* is added to verbs to change them into a noun (for example: *walk – walker*). It can also be added to adjectives to provide further information (for example: *slow – slower*). The ending *est* can also be added to adjectives (for example: *slow – slowest*). The endings *ing* and *ed* are added to verbs to change the tense (for example: *walked* or *walking*).

When it is safe to come out, Tom leaves his shelter and keeps exploring. Wait…is that the cave in the distance?

 1

Write all the words which have an *er, ed, est* or *ing* ending in this passage.

Tom searched long and hard to find Eva's cave, but then he found the greatest cave he could imagine! He now felt like a mighty explorer, ready for all challenges, and he quickly set off looking for ore.

....

2

Tick (✓) the correct word to complete each sentence.

a)   Of all the caves, this one is the

deeper. ☐

deepest. ☐

b)   He

climbed ☐

climbing ☐

a hill to get a better look.

c)   Tom is

looking ☐

looked ☐

for ore.

Tom is almost at the cave entrance. Is he ready for what's inside?

3

Look at the four words below. Think about the different endings it is possible to add to each of them. Write them in whichever columns of the table they can be placed with the ending added on.

great   look   think   help

er ending	*ed* ending	*ing* ending	*est* ending

4

Write your own sentences about exploring the caves. In each sentence, use the word you are given but add an *er*, *ed*, *ing* or *est* ending to it.

a) jump ....

....

b) eat ....

....

c) fast ....

....

d) look ....

....

SPACES AND SENTENCES

Words are often put together in a sentence. Sentences give information, share a thought or ask a question. They keep written and spoken words neat and clear. To help with this, make sure you leave spaces between words when writing.

Tom makes it! The entrance to the cave is big, dark and scary. He will need to be brave to go inside. It is time to start exploring.

Write each of these sentences correctly. Leave spaces between each word.

a) Tom thought he heard azombie.

....

b) There islava in some of the caves.

....

c) Tom cansee some iron ore.

....

Work out what each sentence says. Draw lines to show where there should be spaces between the words.

a) Thecaves aredeep.   b) Tommustnot fall.

c) A llamacanbe tamed.   d) Lava is veryhot.

Tom uses a torch to help him see as he goes deeper inside the cave. There are lots of cobwebs. Stay calm, Tom!

3

Write each set of words in the correct order to form a sentence.

a) cold.   It   quite   is

....

b) There   spider.   a   is

....

c) looks   for   He   ore.

....

4

 Explain what clues you could use in jumbled up sentences to help you put the words into the correct order. Think about how you worked out the answers in question 3. There is another jumbled sentence below to work out.

is   a   This   cave.

....

....

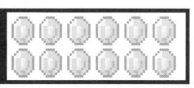

COLOUR IN HOW MANY
EMERALDS YOU EARNED

CAPITAL LETTERS AND FULL STOPS

Every sentence should begin with a capital letter.
Most sentences have a full stop at the end.

Yikes! The spider has seen Tom and starts moving towards him. He gets his sword ready and prepares to fight.

1

Write each of these sentences again. Make sure you use a capital letter and a full stop in your sentences.

a)   tom fought the spider

....

b)   it tried to bite him

....

c)   he swung his sword

....

2

Tick (✓) the two sentences below that have the correct punctuation.

caves are dangerous.   ☐

Tom is good at fighting.   ☐

The spider crawled up the wall.   ☐

Tom must be careful   ☐

Tom hears scary hisses from behind him. More spiders are coming! This fight just got much more dangerous.

3

Circle each mistake or missing punctuation in the sentences below.

a) Tom is ready to fight

b) he needs his sword.

c) Spiders are nasty

d) the cave is huge.

e) He can't see very far

f) it is a spooky place.

4

Here are four sentence parts. Match the sentence parts correctly to create two sentences. Write the two sentences on the lines below.

deep underground.	Be careful or
you could fall.	He is really

....

....

COLOUR IN HOW MANY EMERALDS YOU EARNED

MORE CAPITAL LETTERS

Capital letters are also used for names of people, places, days of the week and months of the year. When using *I* (for example: *I am running*), the *I* is always a capital letter. Titles of books, films and games also begin with a capital letter.

Would Tom survive against the spiders? He thinks of his friend waiting back at the house.

1

Write each of these sentences again using a capital letter for the name.

a)   Here is tom.

b)   This is eva.

....

....

2

Tick (✓) the sentence that has the correct punctuation.

tom is an exciting Minecraft character.   ☐

Tom is an Exciting Minecraft character.   ☐

Tom is a exciting minecraft character.   ☐

Tom is an exciting Minecraft character.   ☐

Tom fights bravely and defeats lots of spiders. It looks like he will win this fight. What a fantastic fighter he is!

3

Write this sentence again using capital letters correctly.

i know tom always practises combat on saturday and sunday.

....

4

Place a tick (✓) underneath each correctly used capital letter. Place a cross (✗) underneath any letter where a capital letter is missing or has been used incorrectly and write the correct letter.

a)   Tom had Beaten all the spiders.

b)   he carried on Deeper into the cave.

c)   It is lucky that Tom is a brave explorer.

USING *AND* TO JOIN WORDS AND SENTENCES

The word *and* is used to join words or sentences together.
For example: *I find some villagers. I trade with them.* →
I find some villagers <u>and</u> I trade with them.

Tom slips and falls into a large cavern which has lots of lava. On the other side of the lava, he spots some precious diamond ore.

1

Write the word *and* in the correct place. Then say each sentence.

a) Tom has escaped from zombies .... spiders.

b) The caves are dark .... deep.

c) There are blocks of diamond ore .... cobblestone.

2

The word *and* is missing in each of these sentences. Write each sentence again, putting the word *and* in the correct place.

a) Tom Eva know how to find the best caves.

....

b) There is a lot of lava obsidian.

....

Tom climbs over to the diamond ore and gets out his pickaxe. Balancing high above the lava, he gets to work.

3

Join the two sentences together with the word *and*. Here is an example to show you what to do:

Tom is climbing high. He is mining the diamond ore.

Tom is climbing high and he is mining the diamond ore.

a)   There are many blocks of ore. He can see the pool of lava.

....

b)   Spiders are scary. Creepers are dangerous.

....

4

Complete each sentence by adding the word *and* with your own ending.

a)   Tom put the diamonds in his inventory ....

....

b)   Tom loves exploring ....

....

QUESTION MARKS

A question mark is the punctuation used at the end of a question sentence. It is used instead of a full stop in these types of sentence.

1

Read and say each sentence below. Add a full stop or a question mark to each.

a) Where is Tom going next ☐

b) He has explored the cave ☐

c) Will he see any zombies ☐

2

Tick (✓) the sentence below that is correctly punctuated.

Will Tom get home safely.
☐

Let's hope Tom gets home safely?
☐

Can Tom get home safely?
☐

Is Tom safe.
☐

Tom mines lots of precious diamonds but now he must find a way out of the lava cave. Answer these questions to help him.

3

Explain what is wrong with each sentence below.

What is Tom doing.

How will he escape from the cave.

Will he see zombies.

....

....

4

Read each answer then think of a question that would give that answer.

Answer   **Question**

a) These are zombies.   ....

b) Tom is in a cave.   ....

c) Tom has fought a spider.   ....

EXCLAMATION MARKS

Exclamation sentences are sentences that show surprise or excitement. They are punctuated with an exclamation mark.

Tom digs through the rock and earth as he tries to make a tunnel back to the surface. Answer these questions to make it easier for him.

 1

Add an exclamation mark to the end of each sentence.

a) Tom fell into a deep hole

b) What a wonderful cave it was

c) Suddenly he saw a bat

d) How amazing this adventure is

 2

Tick (✓) the two sentences that correctly use the exclamation mark.

What a dangerous fight that was! ☐

Can Tom find his way out! ☐

How incredible the caves look! ☐

Will he reach the surface quickly! ☐

Finally, Tom breaks through a wall and is back into the sunshine again. Fresh air at last. How good that feels!

3

Complete each sentence by adding a suitable ending and an exclamation mark.

a) What a terrible ....

b) How amazing ....

4

Read each sentence and complete it with either a full stop, a question mark or an exclamation mark.

a) Tom suddenly saw some incredible emerald ore ☐

b) Had he fought lots of spiders ☐

c) The caves were dark but Tom did not mind ☐

d) What an amazing day it had been ☐

e) What would he and Eva do next ☐

COLOUR IN HOW MANY EMERALDS YOU EARNED

CORRECTING YOUR WORK

It can be easy to make mistakes in your writing, but don't worry. Checking your sentences will help you to put things right.

Tom rushes back across the plains to Eva's house. He can't wait to share the story of his scary cave adventure.

1

Correct the spelling and punctuation in the sentences below. Write the correct spelling or punctuation beneath the place it should go.

a) it was a great adventure so far?

b) It was hard work but tom had escaped the cave

c) What challenges will he mee in the next adventure.

2

Read and say each sentence. Then underline the incorrect word. Write the correct word in the space provided.

a) Tom is explore the caves. ....

b) When Tom fall he hurt himself. ....

c) He was looked at a spider. ....

d) Bats can move fast than creepers. ....

COLOUR IN HOW MANY EMERALDS YOU EARNED

ADVENTURE ROUND-UP

SPARKLING RESULT

Eva is waiting for Tom when he arrives. She can't wait to hear about his adventure in the cave. She can't believe her eyes when he shows her all the diamonds he has mined from the lava cave!

WHERE NEXT?

They have enough diamonds to craft armour and weapons for their next adventure. Tom wants to know where they should explore next. Eva smiles and points to the mountains in the distance. Tom smiles and gets to work on the gear they will need.

COMPOSITION

MOUNTAIN MISSION

The mighty, mysterious snowy mountains are a test for any adventurer. You need to be fast on your feet to climb these giddy heights. Trees are harder to find the higher you climb, so building a shelter can be tricky if you are not prepared.

WATCH YOUR STEP!

You need to be especially careful when battling mobs this high up – one wrong move and you are in for a nasty fall!

TEAMING UP TO GET TO THE TOP

After enjoying their separate adventures, Eva and Tom are going to work together to climb the distant mountain. What will they find at the top?

COMPOSING SENTENCES

Before writing a sentence, make sure you know what you are going to say. Saying the sentence aloud helps to make sure it sounds correct and sends the message you want it to give.

This is going to be an epic expedition. Tom and Eva have to make sure they take plenty of food and equipment.

1

Look at each picture. Think of a short sentence for that picture and say it out loud. When your sentence sounds right, write it in the space provided.

a)

....

....

....

b)

....

....

....

2

Think of a suitable ending to each sentence below. Before you write the ending, say the whole sentence out loud to make sure it sounds correct.

a) Tom and Eva ....

b) The mountain was ....

INFORMATION TEXTS

An information text can be about almost anything. It will include facts and will often explain something new to the reader.

Tom and Eva are at the mountain and are up for another adventure!

1

Look at the picture above. Think of and say two sentences which give facts about the picture. When you have said the sentences aloud, try to write them too.

....

....

2

Complete each sentence by adding the correct missing words. Say the sentence aloud before writing the words in the sentence.

There is snow	Tom admiring	near to the

a) The picture shows .... the mountain.

b) There is a llama .... trees.

c) .... on top of the mountain.

Tom and Eva start to climb the mountain using their pickaxes.

3

Here are three pieces of information about mountains:

| stone surface | snow on top | coal ore in mountains |

Say, then write, a full sentence for each piece of information.

....

....

....

....

....

4

Write two sentences which give survival information about exploring the mountains. Think of each sentence and say it aloud before you write it.

....

....

....

....

COLOUR IN HOW MANY EMERALDS YOU EARNED

47

GIVING INSTRUCTIONS

Sentences are sometimes needed to give instructions. An instruction tells the reader what to do. A good sentence can make the instruction very clear so that it is easy to understand.

As they climb and chip away at the stone blocks, Eva makes a hole that reveals a mysterious cavern – and a spider rushes out!

1

Draw lines to join each instruction sentence to the correct picture.

Do not break your pickaxe.

Look for coal ore in the cavern.

Fight the spider now, Tom!

2

Tick (✓) the two sentences below which are instructions.

The mountain is tall. ☐

You must climb carefully, Eva. ☐

They saw a spider. ☐

Climb the mountain now, Tom. ☐

The spider is going to attack and more spiders are starting to come out of the cavern. Think fast, Eva and Tom!

 3

Think of instruction sentences for each idea below. Say each sentence aloud before you write it.

a) Tell Eva to fight the spider.

....

b) Tell Tom to seal up the cavern.

....

4

 Think of two instructions to help somebody craft a stone pickaxe.

Say your sentences aloud and check they make sense before writing them.

....

....

....

SEQUENCING SENTENCES

When writing, sentences need to be in the correct order to help the reader understand the text. If the end of a story came before the beginning, it would be very confusing. If instructions are written in the wrong order, they become difficult to follow.

Phew! After escaping from the spiders, Eva and Tom make a campfire and have a rest, thinking back over their adventures.

1

Read the sentences and write 1, 2 and 3 in the boxes below to put them in the correct order.

They started to climb and found a mysterious cavern.	Tom and Eva left home on another adventure.	Soon, they arrived in the mountains.
☐	☐	☐

2

Here are some of the things that have happened to Eva and Tom on their adventures. Tick (✓) the sentence which is out of sequence.

More and more spiders came out to attack them. ☐

They managed to escape from the spiders. ☐

Tom and Eva finally relaxed beside their campfire. ☐

Eva made a hole which opened a spider-filled cavern. ☐

Sitting by the fire, Eva tells Tom about a nightmare she had. In the nightmare, she fell off the top of a snowy mountain.

 3

Complete each sentence below to tell a story about Eva climbing the mountain, standing in the snow at the top, and then falling off.

Eva started to ....

At the top she ....

Eva then slipped and ....

4

Look at the three pictures from Tom and Eva's adventure. Say and then write at least one sentence for each picture, retelling the story in that order.

....

....

....

PLANNING A STORY

When planning a story, think about who it will be about and what they will do. This will help to make sure the events are in the correct order.

As they set off again up the mountain, Eva gives Tom some tips about how to tell a good story.

 I

Think about a story you know. Explain to an adult what happens at the beginning of the story, what happens next (the middle of the story) and what happens at the end of the story. You could write a few key ideas down too.

Story title: ....

Beginning	Middle	End

2

Look at the pictures below. The pictures show a character (who will be in the story), a setting (where the story takes place) and an event (something that happens). Describe what you see in each picture and say your sentences aloud. You could also write a few words to describe the picture.

....

....

....

It gets colder as they climb higher up the mountain. Tom has a furnace but they need to find more coal to use it.

3

Look at the pictures below. They show the beginning, the middle and the end of a story. Talk about what is happening in each picture, then try to write each idea down.

....

....

....

....

4

Think of a story involving fire. Answer these questions about your idea, then try to tell the story to somebody.

a) Who is the main character?

....

b) Where is the story set?

....

c) What happens at the beginning?

....

....

d) What happens next?

....

....

e) How does the character feel?

....

f) How does the story end?

....

COLOUR IN HOW MANY EMERALDS YOU EARNED

COMPOSITION

TELLING A STORY 1

Storytelling requires lots of ideas and lots of description. Characters, settings and events need to be described carefully.

While Tom is mining for coal, Eva spots a creeper coming!

1

Look at each picture. Say a sentence or two about the character in the picture. You could write the sentences too.

 a) ....

....

 b) ....

....

 c) ....

....

2

Say and write a sentence for these story settings (where it happens).

a)

b)

....

....

54

Eva stops the creeper and breathes a sigh of relief. Tom can keep mining while you answer the next question.

3

Look at each picture below. Tell somebody a very simple story for each picture. Try to write down your story too.

Example:

Tom was on a snowy mountain. Two zombies appeared so Tom made a snow golem to help fight them. Tom was happy to defeat the zombies.

 a)

b)

TELLING A STORY 2

When writing a story, all the different parts have to come together.

The sun is setting and it is starting to snow. Tom quickly hollows out a shelter and crafts a door and two beds. Eva tells him a bedtime story about what might happen next on their adventure.

Here are pictures of Eva and Tom on their mountain adventure.

a) Say and write two sentences describing Eva and Tom, to follow on from the first line of this story:

One day, Eva and Tom decided to go on a mountain adventure.

....

....

....

b) Say and write the next two sentences of the story, describing the mountains.

....

....

....

Tom wonders what they will find at the top of the mountain. That gives Eva an idea for the next part of her bedtime story.

2

In Eva's story, they climb the mountain but are attacked by an Enderman. Read the first sentence of this part of the story:

Eva and Tom climbed higher and higher up the mountain.

a) Think of a sentence to explain that they were attacked by an Enderman. The first word is given.

Suddenly ....

b) Now think of a sentence which explains that they fought the Enderman and escaped.

....

....

3

How will Eva's story end? They might get to the top of the mountain and see a wonderful view. Or they might find some emerald ore and take it back home. You decide, but remember to say your sentences aloud before you write them.

....

....

....

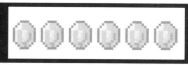

WRITING OTHER TEXTS

Remember that information and instructions need to make sense when you write them. For instructions, it is also important that they are in the correct order. Sentences should follow on from each other.

Eva's story scares Tom so much that he cannot sleep!
What if they really do meet an Enderman?

1

Use the sentence starters below to write short instructions for how to escape an Enderman by throwing water at it.

First ....

Next ....

Finally ....

2

Think of, say and write three sentences about what the mountains are like at night. Try to describe what you might see and hear, and how you might feel.

....

....

....

....

....

....

COLOUR IN HOW MANY EMERALDS YOU EARNED

ADVENTURE ROUND-UP

AN AMAZING DISCOVERY

The next morning, Tom and Eva bravely continue their climb to the top of the mountain. To Tom's relief, there is no Enderman waiting for them. Instead, they find a ruined portal with a treasure chest. Shaking with excitement, they open it and find an enchanted golden helmet! What amazing loot! What an incredible adventure!

PORTAL POSSIBILITIES

The two friends look at the eerie ruined portal. They know that portals allow you to explore dark and dangerous realms beyond this one. Will they be brave enough to build a portal of their own? That is a quest for another day!

ANSWERS

Pages 5–7

1. a) make   b) plains
   c) day   d) safe   [1 emerald each]
2. a) see   b) eat
   c) these   d) thief   [1 emerald each]
3. It will go dark at <u>night</u>.
   Eva will need somewhere to <u>lie</u> down.
   She has <u>tried</u> to craft a bed.
   The villagers are busy with their own <u>lives</u>.
      [1 emerald each]
4. a) biome   b) goal
   c) foe   d) borrow   [1 emerald each]
5. a) cube   b) few
   c) blue   d) food   [1 emerald each]
6. a) r<u>ai</u>n   b) h<u>ome</u>
   c) s<u>ea</u>   d) s<u>igh</u>t   [1 emerald each]

Pages 8–9

1. shirt – ir   verb – er
   turn – ur   her – er   [1 emerald each]
2. a) first   b) survive
   c) bird   d) stronger   [1 emerald each]
3. a) hurt   b) alert
   c) circles   d) expert   [1 emerald each]
4. Long er sound: shirt, survival, occur, person, disturb
   Lazy er sound: under, spider, creeper, shelter, stronger
      [1 emerald each]
5. The answer should acknowledge that the lazy er sound occurs at the end of the words.   [1 emerald]

Pages 10–11

1. (From top left, left to right): Monday, Thursday, Wednesday, Sunday, Tuesday, Friday, Saturday
      [1 emerald each]
2. (From top to bottom): Tuesday, Wednesday, Friday, Sunday   [1 emerald each]
3. a) Monday   b) Friday
   c) Sunday   d) Tuesday
   e) Thursday   f) Saturday
   g) Wednesday   [1 emerald each]
4. a) Tuesday   b) Thursday
   c) Wednesday   d) Monday   [1 emerald each]
5. Accept either: A consonant / A capital letter
      [1 emerald]

Pages 12–13

1. morning   for   ore   before   more   [1 emerald each]
2. ore words: score, shore
   aw words: draw, dawn
   au words: pause, haunt   [1 emerald each]

3. a) ore   b) torch
   c) horses   d) sword   [1 emerald each]
4. Eva <u>**saw**</u> a zombie. It <u>**wore**</u> <u>**torn**</u> clothes. Although she was <u>**short**</u> of strength, she took her <u>**sword**</u> and defeated the zombie. She hoped <u>**more**</u> would not <u>**spawn**</u> nearby.   [1 emerald each]

Pages 14–15

1. a) started   b) arm
   c) scar   d) hard   [1 emerald each]
2. a) lair   b) scare
   c) wear   d) aware   [1 emerald each]
3. air words: fair, pair
   are words: share, scare
   ear words: tear, bear   [1 emerald each]
4. Sometimes it can be <u>**hard**</u> to find food. Eva <u>**stared**</u> at the land ahead of her. <u>**Apart**</u> from a few horses, she could see nothing else. She was so low on health that she <u>**dared**</u> not fight a zombie or a creeper. She then saw a <u>**large**</u> spider. She didn't think this was very <u>**fair**</u> and she realised she was <u>**scared**</u>.   [1 emerald each]

Pages 16–17

1. Eva could hear the **sound** of a skeleton.
   She needed to find shelter **now**.
   It was **about** time she got to safety.
   She looked **around** for somewhere.   [1 emerald each]
2. a) brown   b) outpost
   c) cow   d) down   [1 emerald each]
3. a) f<u>ou</u>nd   b) ar<u>ou</u>nd
   c) <u>out</u>   d) w<u>ow</u>ed   [1 emerald each]
4. a)–d) Each word must be used correctly in a sentence.   [1 emerald each]

Pages 18–19

1. nearby, hear   [1 emerald each]
2. air sound words: where, there
   ear sound as in dear: beard, here, hear, sphere
      [1 emerald each]
3. a) where   b) here
   c) near   d) there   [1 emerald each]
4. Eva could <u>**hear**</u> more creepers <u>**nearby**</u>. She looked but they <u>**were**</u> <u>**nowhere**</u> to be seen.
      [1 emerald each]

Pages 20–21

1. live – v, pull – l, snatch – tch, honk – nk, fizz – z, crack – k, welly – ee   [1 emerald each]
2. a) think   b) have
   c) off   d) catch   [1 emerald each]
3. -ss ending: She heard a <u>**hiss**</u>.

-ll ending: Eva ran up a **hill**.

-ff ending: The creepers were far **off** now.

-ck ending: She tried to **trick** the creepers.

[1 emerald each]

4 a)–d) Each word must be used correctly in a
sentence. [1 emerald each]

Page 22

1 whiff – wh, phonics – ph, king – k, dolphin – ph,
wheel – wh, sketch – k [1 emerald each]

2 a) What   b) skin
   c) which   d) Phew [1 emerald each]

Page 25

1 a) creepers   b) witches
   c) bats   d) blocks [1 emerald each]

2 a) llama   b) trees   c) zombies
[1 emerald each]

Pages 26–27

1 a) unhappy   b) untidy
   c) undo   d) untie [1 emerald each]

2 a) unwell   b) unsure
   c) unable   d) unlucky [1 emerald each]

3 a) unseen   b) unlike
   c) unknown   d) unfair [1 emerald each]

4 Correct *un-* words: unlock, untie, unfold, unusual
Incorrect *un-* words: unagree, unappear, uncorrect
[1 emerald each]

Pages 28–29

1 searched, greatest, explorer, looking [1 emerald each]

2 a) deepest   b) climbed
   c) looking [1 emerald each]

3 *er* ending: greater, looker, thinker, helper
[1 emerald for two or more correct]
ed ending: looked, helped [1 emerald for both correct]
ing ending: looking, thinking, helping
[1 emerald for two or more correct]
est ending: greatest [1 emerald]

4 Each word must be used correctly in a sentence.
[1 emerald each]
   a) jumped, jumper or jumping must be used
   b) eating or eater must be used
   c) faster or fastest must be used, but accept fasted
   or fasting if used correctly
   d) looker, looked or looking must be used

Pages 30–31

1 a) Tom thought he heard a zombie. [1 emerald]
   b) There is lava in some of the caves. [1 emerald]
   c) Tom can see some iron ore. [1 emerald]

2 a) The|caves are|deep. [1 emerald]
   b) Tom|must|not fall. [1 emerald]
   c) A llama|can|be tamed. [1 emerald]
   d) Lava is very|hot. [1 emerald]

3 a) It is quite cold. [1 emerald]
   b) There is a spider. [1 emerald]
   c) He looks for ore. [1 emerald]

4 Unjumbled sentence: This is a cave. [1 emerald]
An acknowledgement that the capital letter and full
stop are clues for the ordering. [1 emerald]

Pages 32–33

1 a) Tom fought the spider.
   b) It tried to bite him.
   c) He swung his sword. [1 emerald each for the
   capital letter and full stop in each sentence.]

2 Tom is good at fighting. [1 emerald]
Tom|must|not fall.
The spider crawled up the wall. [1 emerald]

3 a) Missing full stop [1 emerald]
   b) Capital letter needed at the beginning of the
   sentence [1 emerald]
   c) Missing full stop [1 emerald]
   d) Capital letter needed at the beginning of the
   sentence [1 emerald]
   e) Missing full stop [1 emerald]
   f) Capital letter needed at the beginning of the
   sentence [1 emerald]

4 Be careful or you could fall. [1 emerald]
He is really deep underground. [1 emerald]

Pages 34–35

1 a) Here is Tom. [1 emerald]
   b) This is Eva. [1 emerald]

2 Tom is an exciting Minecraft character. [1 emerald]

3 **I** know **T**om always practises combat on **S**aturday
and **S**unday. [1 emerald each]

4 a) **T**om had **B**eaten all the spiders.
   ✓   ✗ (b) [1 emerald each]
   b) **h**e carried on **D**eeper into the cave.
   ✗ (H)   ✗ (d) [1 emerald each]
   c) **I**t is lucky that **T**om is a brave explorer.
   ✓   ✓ [1 emerald each]

Pages 36–37

1 Ensure *and* is added to each sentence and that the
sentence is read clearly.
   a) Tom has escaped from zombies **and** spiders.
[1 emerald]
   b) The caves are dark **and** deep. [1 emerald]
   c) There are blocks of diamond ore **and**
   cobblestone. [1 emerald]

2 a) Tom **and** Eva know how to find the best caves.
[1 emerald]
   b) There is a lot of lava **and** obsidian. [1 emerald]

3 a) There are many blocks of ore **and** he can see the
   pool of lava. [1 emerald]
   b) Spiders are scary **and** creepers are dangerous.
[1 emerald]

4. **a)–b)** Each sentence starter must be followed by the word *and* and have an appropriate ending related to the first part of the sentence.

[I emerald each]

Pages 38–39

1 **a)** ? **b)** . **c)** ?

[I emerald each]

2 Can Tom get home safely? [I emerald]

3 The answer should acknowledge that each sentence requires a question mark rather than a full stop at the end. [I emerald]

4 Any appropriate question sentences (which must end in a question mark).

Examples:
a) What are these?
b) Where is Tom?
c) Has Tom had a fight? [I emerald each]

Pages 40–41

1 Each sentence should have a correctly added exclamation mark at the end.
a) Tom fell into a deep hole! [I emerald]
b) What a wonderful cave it was! [I emerald]
c) Suddenly he saw a bat! [I emerald]
d) How amazing this adventure is! [I emerald]

2 What a dangerous fight that was! [I emerald]
How incredible the caves look! [I emerald]

3 Any appropriate exclamation sentences (which must end in an exclamation mark).

Examples:
a) What a terrible cave that was! [I emerald]
b) How amazing Tom's sword skills are! [I emerald]

4 **a)** ! (or .) **b)** ? **c)** .
d) ! **e)** ? [I emerald each]

Page 42

1 **a)** It was a great adventure so far. [I emerald each]
b) It was hard work but Tom had escaped the cave.

[I emerald each]

c) What challenges will he **meet** in the next adventure? [I emerald each]

2 **a)** explore – exploring [I emerald]
(also accept changing *is* to an appropriate word, e.g. *can/cannot, will, would, should*)
b) fall – fell [I emerald]
c) looked – looking [I emerald]
(also accept changing *was* to *had* or *has*)
d) fast – faster [I emerald]

Page 45

1 **a)–b)** The spoken sentence is the most important aspect here. The child should also be encouraged to write the sentence, ensuring a capital letter and the correct final punctuation is used. [I emerald each]

2 **a)–b)** A meaningful sentence should be spoken and written (ensure end punctuation is in place).

[I emerald each]

Pages 46–47

1 Two meaningful, spoken sentences related to the picture. The child should also be encouraged to write the sentences, ensuring a capital letter and the correct final punctuation is used. [I emerald for each sentence]

2 **a)** Tom admiring **b)** near to the
c) There is snow [I emerald each]

3 Ensure the sentences relate to the information provided, and ensure that the spoken sentences are discussed as necessary before writing.

[I emerald for each sentence]

4 Each sentence should be correctly constructed and initially said aloud. Each sentence must provide survival information about exploring the mountains.

[I emerald for each sentence]

Example answer:
Be careful that you do not fall. It is cold in the snow.

Pages 48–49

1 Do not break your pickaxe.

Look for coal ore in the cavern.

Fight the spider now, Tom!

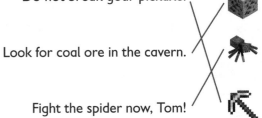

[I emerald each]

2 You must climb carefully, Eva. [I emerald]
Climb the mountain now, Tom. [I emerald]

3 **Example answers:**
a) Fight the spider, Eva. [I emerald]
b) You must seal up the cavern, Tom. [I emerald]

4 Each sentence should be correctly constructed and initially said aloud. Each sentence must provide an instruction for crafting a stone pickaxe.

Example answer:
Mine three cobblestone blocks and craft two wooden planks into sticks. Use these items to craft the stone pickaxe.

[I emerald for each sentence]

Pages 50–51

1 They started to climb and found a mysterious cavern. 3
Tom and Eva left home on another adventure. 1
Soon, they arrived in the mountains. 2

[I emerald each]

2 Eva made a hole which opened a spider-filled cavern.
[1 emerald]

3 Each sentence must be completed with relevant information related to Eva on the mountain. Each sentence must make sense and include the correct final punctuation.
Example sentences:
Eva started to **climb the mountain.**
At the top she **stood in the snow.**
Eva then slipped and **fell off the mountain.**
[1 emerald for each sentence]

4 Each sentence must be linked to the pictures and in order. Each sentence must make sense and include the correct punctuation.
Example sentences:
Tom and Eva were mining for ore.
They had a fight with spiders.
They made a campfire.   [1 emerald for each sentence]

Pages 52–53

1 Discuss a story known to the child.   [1 emerald for provision of information for each part of the story (beginning, middle and end)]

2 Verbal descriptions (encourage full sentences) should be given for each picture.   [1 emerald each]

3 Verbal descriptions should be given for each picture. Encourage full sentences which follow on from each other.   [1 emerald each]

4 **a)–f)** Ensure that the answers make sense. Discuss them with your child.   [1 emerald each]

Pages 54–55

1 **a)–c)** Verbal sentences should be given about each character. Encourage full sentences, discuss each character and encourage writing of the sentences once discussed.   [1 emerald each]

2 **a)–b)** Encourage full sentences, and discuss each setting before the final sentences are said aloud and then written.   [1 emerald each]

3 **a)–b)** For each part, a very simple story (of at least two sentences) in a similar manner to the example given.   [1 emerald each]

Pages 56–57

1 **a)** Two sentences, one about Eva and one about Tom. Ensure these are said aloud and discussed before being written.   [1 emerald]

b) Two sentences describing the mountains. Ensure these are said aloud and discussed before being written.   [1 emerald]

2 **a)** Any sentence which says they were attacked by an Enderman.   [1 emerald]

b) Any sentence which says that they fought the Enderman and escaped.   [1 emerald]

3 Any suitable ending of at least two sentences which follow on from the previous events in the story.
[1 emerald for each sentence up to a maximum of 2]

Page 58

1 Any suitable sentences.
Example answers:
First get some water.   [1 emerald]
Next throw it at the Enderman.   [1 emerald]
Finally run away as quickly as you can.   [1 emerald]

2 Any suitable three sentences which describe the mountains at night. Ensure each sentence is said aloud and discussed, ensuring it makes sense. Each sentence should then be written with the correct punctuation as necessary.
[1 emerald for each sentence]

TRADE IN YOUR EMERALDS!

Congratulations on reaching the end of this amazing Minecraft adventure! You helped Tom and Eva battle scary mobs, mine precious ore and climb a giant mountain. Phew! Now it's time to count up how many emeralds you earned along the way.

Imagine you are setting off on an adventure of your own and trade your gems with the merchant for the things you'll need. What will you choose? If you have enough emeralds, you could buy more than one of some items.

Ask a grown-up to help you count all your emeralds and write the total in this box.

HMMM?

SHOP INVENTORY

- IRON CHESTPLATE: 15 EMERALDS
- IRON LEGGINGS: 12 EMERALDS
- IRON HELMET: 8 EMERALDS
- IRON BOOTS: 6 EMERALDS
- DIAMOND CHESTPLATE: 30 EMERALDS
- DIAMOND LEGGINGS: 24 EMERALDS
- DIAMOND HELMET: 16 EMERALDS
- DIAMOND BOOTS: 12 EMERALDS
- SHIELD: 20 EMERALDS
- BELL: 5 EMERALDS
- ENCHANTED IRON CHESTPLATE: 25 EMERALDS
- ENCHANTED IRON BOOTS: 10 EMERALDS
- ENCHANTED DIAMOND BOOTS: 20 EMERALDS
- ENCHANTED DIAMOND CHESTPLATE: 50 EMERALDS
- ENCHANTED DIAMOND LEGGINGS: 40 EMERALDS

That's a lot of emeralds. Well done! Remember, just like real money, you don't need to spend it all. Sometimes it's good to save up.